REMEMBER ME
BY: Jermaine Wilkins

Future Books
Urban Novels:

Eight Corner Boys
Eight Corner Boys: Rome's Return
Eight Corner Boys: Rome's Demise

Poetry:

Forget About Me

Autobiography:

Enter the Calamity

Remember Me

Remember me when you think of what's real and what's loyal.
What's just and fair?

Remember me when things of troubled times and despair are mentioned, when torment is talked about.

Remember me when you think of a rider when you think of dependability.
When you think of love.

Remember me when you think of putting in work or needing someone to give you a hug.

Talking about a man in big shoes with a heart bigger than the planet that we live on.

Remember me on the day that your kid was born.

Remember me for all time and in all thoughts of a man intertwined between life and death for if you remember all of the good things about a man you can forget the rest. Even now remember me for remembering me lets my spirit after death live on.

Tic Toc

Why must I sit and sit,
While the clock just ticks and ticks and ticks and tocs and ticks and tocs.

U sit in DOC.'s and still u miss slinging rocks even after the fed's just hit the
spot, you sat and sat despair made you rat and rat, while you rat to cops the clock just
tocs and tocs,

And ticks and tocs and ticks and tocs.

Why would you flee then stop or get knocked the turn over and be the cops,
you was gangster while bagging up green and rocks.

Your whole focus is to bleed the block, while seeing that cream in knots. You
try to count it but lose count for all you hear is the clock,

Tic, tic, Tic, Tocs!
Tic, Tocs

How your dope is? Tell them just be a fiend and cop,
Since that first blast they need to shop similar in the way you think that you
need the block,
But for you it's not just a block thing so you need a spot.
Caught out there slipping so now you got eight holes from four bullets. So now as

you load that glock preparing to put a body in its box you listen for signs that you
may be stopped but all you hear in your mind is,
Tic Tic - Toc Toc - Tic Tic - Tic Toc.

Pockets on E so you plan to scheme if you have to run up and blam the team. So now
you plotted and now you got it, call for that re-up man and tell him how many grams
to bring.

Waiting on him you sit and think how you never smoked but like an addict for this
rock I am a fiend. Just like a fiend you need this rock damn what's the difference.......
Tic Tocs Tic Tocs the clock just stopped.

Life

"Life is full of twists and turns never knowing what lies ahead or what lessons are to be learned. Everyday one seeks a new means of survival. One can never have enough knowledge of how to survive. Life is something that must be dealt with in great care and concern. Life is like the game of chess one must strategies in order to win the final war. This process may be long and frivolous or short and sweet. The is to figure out the best strategy in order to conquer. Once one comes across those bumps we must get across them with great precision. If one can to learn to survive in the streets the one can survive anything. Some survive only to be defeated, and others survive to achieve a greater means. Life is full of all things one can imagine it's what one makes of them that matters. Don't strive for the lesser but instead strive for the greater good."

"Anything that one cherishes one should fight for, for it is better to fight and lose than to never have fought at all. For fighting for what one cherishes and losing is winning in its own right"
-Jermaine Wilkins

No / Yes

No

I will not give in to the death of my people, watching crack-heads commit suicide by pipe and junkies burst their hearts with main line needles.

No

Chance to survive when nobody cares, when you wake up to roach's and rats to the super chasing the homeless away with aluminum bats. Poverty stricken is what we were born, still alive but forced to mourn at the sight of your third baby being born.

No

Chance for a black man in a society that was designed by a white man and built on the back of the black man.

No

Healthcare for the ghetto slums but suburbia is steady prospering and elevating. Charges pending for sending your child to a school out of the limits of your home address. More problems more stress.

Yes

The war is ongoing. Police walk the beat only to be slaughtered but we are to blame when it happens who blames them for the violations that happen to those on the street.

Yes

Politicians corrupt what is right and Priests crush the hopes of those whose minds are so fragile, taking from them the dignity they were born with. Slaps on the wrist for these high figures while at the bottom people serve the extra time they gave back for lesser charges.
Yes
They got to make quota so no bail at Christmas stay in until the New Year.

Yes
We will help to get back our respect, our pride. People live with false hopes we wage a war that is based on a governments bullying of a lesser people.
Yes
This is a money based world and no we will no longer stay tied down when we can stand as one

To My Friend

Among the men that god gave breath you may have been one of the best,
Now we cast your name in stone because our father brought you home.

Nobody mentioned how we once chilled and played or how we'd been so close until
this day. I wasn't there when he did his work but I knew when I felt the hurt.

I have no shame to tell the world your precious name. I will stand in freedom and
testify, on that rock what a wonderful man that God has got.

The list had 10 condemned to life by his side; I only wish you weren't so quick to
ride. When we last spoke I could have never known that our time together was
almost gone.

I sit here now just missing you the strength I have is what gets me through. Never
worry your name lives on in all our minds forever and in this poem. And to say the
least your mothers strong. If I could I would sing a song and if you were here you'd
sing along.

We all must go, we come to live and die. I now feel no sorrow cause I will wake and
you wont tomorrow but at least it's said that you sit up high.

Slave Cabin

A tiny room with one door
One little window

An inmate's bench

Some words that label things
Toilet
In which I relieve myself
Sink
In which I wash
Mirror
So I can see the man that I am and not the boy that I once was
Walls
In which I look and stare and realize my smallest dreams and
My biggest nightmares
Nothing except bricks and cold steel
As I write my bottom aches from the cold chair
No pleasure only pain as I sit and think of a way to beat the white mans game
Hold on Massa's calling
You want rec boy
Got to dip it's my only freedom in this cell full of bricks
I only got one hour to get away from this shit.

White Man

He wants me
Wants my son
Wants my daughter

If he gets them it's gone be slaughter
They think its freedom in this country
Just slavery and torment

What will it cost to get our rights back?
What will it cost to get our lives back?

He says I want you
Let me be your owner
Let me rule your lives
Let me work you
Let me take your daughters
And rape your wives

See me
Smell me
Fear me

I am he

Nobody realizes what you do
He'll never stop

What will it take before we break.........?

Reaction

What is?
What does?
We want
Just cause
He has
We take
Don't temp
Your fate
Why me
You ask
When he
Hand it down
You sit
And frown
But why
Be sick
You knew
It then
Just how this story ends!

Whose Love Do I Have

Whose love do I have?

The love of the block trying to get me drunk and high
As I vomit they sit and laugh
I'm wondering why.

When in jail nobody writes
But when I return its all smiles and bright teeth.

Whose love do I have?

The love of people who condone in what's wrong
Buts never what's right
Always got your back but when my turn comes whose really their for the fight.

Always with that would of
Could have did
Stop
And do what you should have did.

Whose love do I have?

When I need bail

Never come to my rescue
As I sit
And torment in
A cell.
They rather see me in jail
Restless torment
As I sit in a cell.
Whose love do I have?

The love of the C.O.
As I get violated and wait on my P.O.

Whose love do I have?

When I'm doing so much
Got my wife ripping and running
I'm driving her crazy
Not knowing that I'm killing my baby.

When young brothers in the streets cockin
And gunnin
Innocent take
Out running.

Whose love do I have?

When love is
What you make it
Offered five years
And you forced to take it.

Whose love do I have?

Nobodies but my own
That's how real brothers make it!

"Life is not measured by the number of breaths we take- but by the moments that take our breath away"

- Unknown

What Love Be Like?

Who would I expect to understand what love be like?
What love is like?

Like living on a cloud or flying with the stars.

Spending a half life looking for your own love.

Expecting to find love walking down the street in your neighborhood.
Her face toward the sky,
Hoping that she noticed you standing there with that smile shining like the glare in
the sun.

Someone who means something.

Your love! Your care!

Is it you are you the one?
Is it you?
Is it you that's there?

Never could I speak just always stare, the love that you have is oh' so rare.

Cheated

Who has cheated death and cheated life all in one?

Shot up and survived with in inches...
Only to be stabbed, die and brought back only to die again.

Saved only to continue to die
Lives life's lies... Why?

Continue without caution
Prevail by any means...

Tattered and torn
Like a book whose pages are worn...

Look death in the face and never mourn...

Somebody tell me how I've cheated so much yet I'm still scorn!

Special Moments

Special moments come not too often to those of us who are not accustom to good things. Most times we look over our special moments. These times occur when we are too focused on other things. Life is full of special of special moments it's on us to capture the essence of the moments and not let them pass us by. In order to see these moments we must first open our eye's to life and stop being blinded or in some cases blinding ourselves. We must live life's special moments as much as you can because you never know when and which special moment may be your last.

"Because this is a game of predator and prey. The stakes are always perilous you can't figure out why a snake moves the way it does. The key is to recognize and accept the snake for what it is, kill it or avoid it- but never try to be-friend or reform it"

- Socrates

Lies

Lies entrap people's souls keeping them hostage. Lies are gateways to a lesser truth. A truth much lesser than the lies used to conceal that truth. A much lesser truth than the truth we live each day in reality. Lies are created in a realm of imagination. Lies are the solar opposite of truth, Lies are given as a means to conceal truth, a truth that one may or may not want to face. To conceal a feeling or a sense of missing something, to cover a act or way of life.

To conceal truth is to hide truth and to hide is to conceal. So to conceal the truth you must first hide it behind a lie.

Climax

I lick her thighs like a sex fiend
My tongue enters her slowly
My hands reach up and squeeze her breasts
They feel like warm morsels
She tastes like heaven with a strawberry frosting
Her juices fill my mouth a flavor I can't live with out

She caress' me slowly before tasting
She takes pride and care with every bob of her head
Her saliva runs down my shaft
She juggles my balls
Further down
She twirls that enchanting tongue in my ass
I stop her before I have the time to nut

I lay back on the bed
She straddles me
She's wet
Her juices cover me as penetration is made
She moves her body up and down
In precise rhythm not missing a stroke
She moans as the speed increases

I turn her over I'm feeling like a dog
As I enter her she moans
She's coming hard
She pulls me towards her
Deeper, deeper
I pump harder and harder
Her screams get louder
My strokes get faster and faster

Were sweating hard
The sheets are soaked

The strokes are long and hard
Her pussy is soft and wet
She cum's again
I'm almost ready
I want to hold off she wants it now
Its time

I pull out she takes me in her mouth
She pumps me with her hand
I release every drop into her frontal lobe
She sucks the rest out
Remnants still linger around her mouth....

Ass Backwards

I wonder why brothers treat the block ass backwards!

Instead of you watching for cops,
The cops sit on the block and watch them cop...

They say they riding but,
But when you throw a blow they sit back and watch you pop...

Real brothers is what they claim,
But real are me and you just lames...

U should never tell
But these brothers quick to take pen to paper
Fronting like you gangster
When it comes to statements you do explain...

I wonder why brothers treat the block ass backwards!

When you set your down your pack,
They lurking in the cut peeking waiting to pick it up
As soon as you turn your back...

Speaking behind your back

Get violated by a young brother and then
Come running for you like track...

Always take but never give
We can all eat just let a real brother live...
Trying to lay with your chick while you gone
Instead of helping shortie
With the kids at home...

I wonder why brothers treat the block ass backwards!

This goes to show that real brothers are on the brink of extinction while lames, rats
and coward brothers thrive.

That's why I treat the block face forward to keep us real brothers alive!

DEDICATED TO REAL BROTHERS EVERYWHERE

"The black race is a target whether we fail or succeed"
- Unknown

2009

2009 the black man finally took his place in the white house!

Now were leading, no longer being treated and talked to like nothing,
Were somebody
No longer yes siring cleaning up after somebody
Slaves started the dream
Martin died for the dream
Malcolm died for the dream
Plus a bunch of other brothers died in between

The black man speaks and now the white man listens
No-more chopping down trees or sweeping the white mans kitchen

2009 time for change, Freedom bells rang
Not entirely but real close
This is just mere dust in a breeze

We to must play our part
We must stop killing ourselves by being pimps, drug pusher's bank robbers and
thieves

We believe in what's wrong
Now believe in what's right

Believe in the struggle
Believe in the fight
It's started and soon we'll get there have no fear shed no tears cause its 2009 and a
black mans here!

Father

In memory of Arnold E. Smiley

When he left I was a little nigga
Now I'm a little bigga

I am you
You are me

I am who
Who is he?

He is my father!

<u>Why Do They Rat? Why Do They Tell?</u>

Why do they rat? Why do they tell?

Sitting around gossiping with police like a bunch of females, but they not drunk or high from snorting or popping them pills.

They sober as hell ratting to police like that shit is real...

Why do they rat? Why do they tell?

Still trying to figure out that while I sit in this cell.

So called gangsters went from keeping the war on the block to siding with cops. At the start all ya'll was gangsters till you seen that blood shed was a whole lot quicker than your son fled...

Why do they rat? Why do they tell?

Brothers is quick to talk how they dump lead, but
Got brothers sitting in cells or with they legs swinging off the top of a bunk bed.

Walking the streets with wires slapping real brothers up while they work off they time for them bum fed's.

Keep it street when them shells hit, either be man enough to walk away or let them shells rip...

Why do they rat? Why do they tell?
Do-boys and dummies ready to shoot,
But when they get jammed up you give them the boot.
Got real brothers sitting beneath gun towers, Elmira reception mandatory chow, five gallon buckets for one shower,
Wiping toilets or cleaning cashed checks off the wall while the rats in the streets having a ball...

Why do they rat? Why do they tell?

Ill never know because I never rat and I never tell. I'm a real brother and before I do ill do what these rats should do and eat they guns and blow themselves to hell!

"The great danger of having enemies is not what they may do to us - it is what We do to ourselves as we allow anger to develop"
- David Hubbard

<u>Freedom</u>

Freedom from torment, and
Freedom from pain.

So many freedoms are they all the same?

Freedoms that bring us pleasure, and
Freedoms that bring us heartache.

Lovers in freedom,
Lovers insane.

Missing the freedom of life, while
Missing the freedom to live.

The freedom to take, and
The freedom to give.

If we no longer have freedom then how can we LIVE?

Emotions

Sometimes we thought are thoughtless emotions.

Separated by time and space,
Unknown to those un-tame human beings.

Emotions there's thoughts of pleasure, and
Thoughts of pain.

Although were unsure of these thoughtless emotions,
We seek out the thoughts one thinks in his/hers emotions.

Tears

Sometimes tears can erase the pain, and sometimes tears only make the pain worse. Pleasuring tears are the ones that make us smile. There the ones that brightens our day, the ones that one sheds at weddings and babies births. These are of joy and of happiness. These are the tears that make moments special.

Sometimes tears can be the worse thing a person has. They have the ability to open a door of emotion that may be unbearable. It may be to powerful to release. In some cases the emotions being released are the emotions that have built up for some time. These emotions can be helpers or they could be the downfall that plagues us all. Some must learn when and when not to release those tears and hopes that the wrong emotions are not released.

"Anything built on negativity will eventually bring destruction to those who profit from it"

- Azie

A Fathers Loss & a Mothers Sorrow

A father's loss and a mothers sorrow, the pain of a child not seeing tomorrow.

The pain of a child not seeing today, the pain of a child not seeing tonight.

The pain of a child not winning, but losing the fight.

The pain of a wife and mother striving hard to take care of her lover.

The sound of a father desperate to cry,
His countless thoughts as he sits wondering why.

Why stress a mother to the brink?
Why force an unborn baby to die?

Why not sit back and enjoy?
Why not cherish a life?

A father's loss and a mothers sorrow.
A father takes blame because it's his fault that his baby won't ever get to tomorrow!

Self Thoughts

Who knew power was pain
But the pain was the power

To control what we have no control
To see what we are blinded from

To live when death becomes

Write what cannot be spoke
Speak what cannot be wrote

Adopt when adoption is
But a mere glimpse of an option

Take wings and fly
Fly to where?

In this place there is no sky
There is no air

No stairway to Heaven
Only the staircase to Hell

No love just lust
No loyalty
No trust

Take your time
Why speed
No rush
Forget all the freedoms
Only bring the torment
And tag along with the pain

Stay away from joy

Say no to the sunshine
And head towards the rain

Kidnapping kids
Only showing kids how to be kidnapped

It was just a mistake

Could it all be a mishap?

Perhaps I should just cry
Or maybe just die

But if nothing makes sense just ask this.

WHY!

You Left Us

In Loving Memory of Elizabeth Colon

You left us with so much and so plenty
You left us a lifetime of dreams and fond memories
You left us a hope for the future and a brighter day
You left us a meal on the table when we came in too late
You left us the wish that you'll return
You left us with children to hold your memory strong
You left us with that gentle word or that sweet song
You left us for a new world and a better place

You left us but to this day I can still see your face!

"Poverty robs us of options"
- Unknown

Forget Me

Forget me when a lame is mentioned or when shame is mentioned.

Forget me when things of calamity appear or when men run with fear.

Forget me when things of the past are gone.

Forget me when bullets tear through a tattered body.

Forget me when the pages of this book are torn.

Forget me now for I am gone and remembering me will only cause many to mourn.

Family\Friends

What is a friend that stands aside while another friend rides?

What is family that stands by while you enter calamity?

What kind of friend sends a message to an outsider for him to blam at you?

What kind of family will lead you to death, and then walk away when the damage's through?

Torn between family and friends who will be the death of me when this tragedy ends?

<u>Shame</u>

Why would you give me up?
Why would you choose to beat your feet?

You'll never know what you have lost.
You'll only assume what you may have gained.

Those images of you in dreams they never came.
I'd die for my rights and you just signed them over like the title to a car.
You never thought I'd go far, or did I have to far to go?

How can you create a life and play with it like it's a game.
You toyed with me and chose temptation over me and that's a selfish thing.

But as soon as you signed your name you freed me and allowed freedom bells to
ring.

Somehow I've learned to love you somewhere, some how. I always hated you but I
learned that for me to hate I had to become what I hated and I would die before I
stoop to that. I could not hate you for hating you would make me the same.

Never worry there's no cause for alarm or pain. There's only sunshine in my skies
you were the rain. I do want you to know that when our paths cross again I will ask
one thing of you "LOOK ME IN THE EYES AND SEE IF YOU SEE THE

SHAME"

Alemap

What words could explain Alemap?
What is this?
What does it stand for?

Alemap is...

These words that describe her: Real Loving Mother Sister Aunt Friend Go Getter
Boss Survivor at all cost....

Alemap is a woman of great magnitude and stature. She preaches but her words are
from the pastors and even further from the masters.

She saves when she is the victim and smiles when all fails to and wins when none
prevails to.

She's a team leader but no coach.
She sat down without being down to sit.
Society's statistics bitten but never was she ridden just forgiving.
Rider is she and who else but he is that, which she rides for.
A better life is none other that what she strives for.

Alemap is special without cause, no reason just cause.
All giving and beautiful.

Precious from the roots of her hair to the tips of her cuticles.
Ever tending with no pause.

Alemap is full of hustle and heart,
More than many and,
Fewer could play her part.
Alemap is a woman who feeds with no cause, rides with no balls and stands when all
else falls, waiting on the reticule to stall...

Mostly Alemap stands for hope for us all!

Atnahs

Atnahs my heart my soul we've been dealt bad hands and we never fold.

This tale of Atnahs will never grow old
Meeting in a way that felt destined to be or
In a way that feels destined to me or
Maybe destined for us

Atnahs to me is destined for trust
Passion creates great love, why lust
Cooking cleaning as Atnahs does
She'll never change causing me to remember what Atnahs was

What is Atnahs?

Atnahs was and is me, what keeps me from insanity or tormenting the streets with calamity and chaos.

Atnahs is a heart that beats forever,
Atnahs cannot die for in my heart
She lives ever so high

Atnahs gave love when I hadn't the slightest reason or care
She stood by me when I was unfair

Torn feelings is Atnahs
Bruised skin mixed with pride is Atnahs
Wanting something better for me is Atnahs

Shining in the darkest sky is Atnahs
Holding a priceless value Atnahs is a masterpiece
Queen to me but not cherished
She is quick to stand and slower to fall

Atnahs is cherished by me,
Even when the charity Atnahs cannot always see

But my love is what Atnahs will always be!

Special Thanks:

I want to thank a few people for the inspiration with this book and to whom this book is dedicated. First off I want to thank my higher power who is secretly there through everything I go through and just as importantly "I WANT TO THANK THE STREETS FOR GIVING ME GRIND THAT I HAVE CASUE THE BEST HUSTLE COMES FRESH OUT OF THE GUTTER". I want to thank my mom Crecy who I love with all my heart and who always wants the best for me in all aspects of life even though we don't always see eye to eye. Thanks to my big cousin **Pam** for always keeping a roof over my head and looking out for me. I love you like my mom cousin. **To Wally, Paris, Veek, Bebo, Hammer, Willis, Paul, Lil Mark and Pepto.** Roc City stand up. To the person who thought up this whole book idea **V. Secrets** baby what's good sweetheart. To all the enemies and hater's I'm not mad but grateful so good looking even you lames had something to do with this. **To every and anybody that ever had encouraging words to say to me in my life.** One person gave me the most will and strive to put the word in this book together and that's **Terrie Lynn Wilkins** if it wasn't for your downfall I could never have come up. And that's REAL!!

And to those who I've met along the years and in all my walks of life. Thank-you.
Weld Block-Eight Corner Inc-Grind Digital

www.ingramcontent.com/pod-product-compliance
Lightning Source LLC
Chambersburg PA
CBHW071740020426
42331CB00008B/2114